I Am Rosa Parks

BY ROSA PARKS

WITH JIM HASKINS • ILLUSTRATED BY WIL CLAY

PUFFIN BOOKS

To my lovely granddaughter
Tamika Clay

JB Parks

PUFFIN BOOKS
Published by the Penguin Group
Penguin Putnam Books for Young Readers, 345 Hudson Street, New York, New York 10014, U.S.A.
Penguin Books Ltd, 80 Strand, London WC2R ORL, England
Penguin Books Australia Ltd, Ringwood, Victoria, Australia
Penguin Books Canada Ltd, 10 Alcorn Avenue, Toronto, Ontario, Canada M4V 3B2
Penguin Books (N.Z.) Ltd, 182-190 Wairau Road, Auckland 10, New Zealand

Penguin Books Ltd, Registered Offices: Harmondsworth, Middlesex, England

First published in the United States of America by Dial Books for Young Readers,
a division of Penguin Books USA Inc., 1997
Published by Puffin Books, a member of Penguin Putnam Books for Young Readers, 2000

15 16 17 18 19 20

Portrait of Mrs. Parks with children on p. 45 is based on a photograph © Monica Morgan/Monica Morgan
Photography. Painting on p. 40 is based on a photograph used with permission of the Bettman Archives.
Painting on p. 41 is based on a photograph used with permission of the SCLC.

THE LIBRARY OF CONGRESS HAS CATALOGED THE DIAL EDITION AS FOLLOWS:
Parks, Rosa, date
I am Rosa Parks/by Rosa Parks with Jim Haskins; pictures by Wil Clay.—1st ed.   p. cm.
Summary: The black woman whose acts of civil disobedience led to the 1956 Supreme Court order
to desegregate buses in Montgomery, Alabama, explains what she did and why.
ISBN 0-8037-1206-5 (trade).—ISBN 0-8037-1207-3 (lib. bdg.)
1. Parks, Rosa, date—Juvenile literature. 2. Afro-Americans—Alabama—Montgomery—Biography—Juvenile
literature. 3. Civil rights workers—Alabama—Montgomery—Biography—Juvenile literature. 4. Afro-Americans—
Civil rights—Alabama—Montgomery—Juvenile literature. 5. Segregation in transportation—Alabama—
Montgomery—History—20th century—Juvenile literature. 6. Montgomery (Ala.)—Race relations—
Juvenile literature. 7. Montgomery (Ala.)—Biography—Juvenile literature. [1. Parks, Rosa, date
2. Civil rights workers. 3. Afro-Americans—Biography.] I. Haskins, James, date. II. Clay, Wil, ill. III. Title.
F334.M753P37 1997 976.1'4700496073—dc20 96-896 CIP AC

Puffin Easy-to-Read ISBN 0-14-130710-2
Puffin® and Easy-to-Read® are registered trademarks of Penguin Putnam Inc.

Printed in the United States of America

Reading Level 2.2

CONTENTS

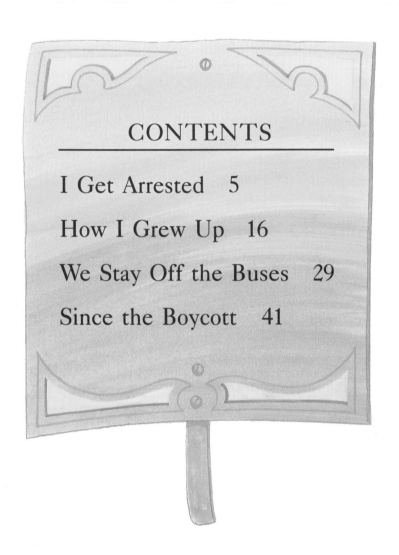

I GET ARRESTED

Many years ago

black people in the South

could not go to the same schools

as white people.

We could not eat in white restaurants.

We could not even drink

from the same water fountains.

We had to stay apart

from white people

everywhere we went.

This was called segregation.

Segregation was the law in the South.

If we broke the law,

we could be arrested, or hurt,

or even killed.

When we rode a bus,

we could only sit in the back seats.

The front seats

were just for white people.

If all the front seats were filled

with white people,

we black people

had to give up our seats

to the next white people

who got on the bus.

That's the way we rode the buses
in the South when I was younger.
I rode the buses and obeyed the laws
that kept me apart from white people.
But I did not think they were right.

One day I was riding on a bus.
I was sitting in one of the seats
in the back section for black people.
The bus started to get crowded.
The front seats filled up
with white people.
One white man was standing up.

The bus driver looked back

at us black people sitting down.

The driver said,

"Let me have those seats."

He wanted us to get up

and give our seats to white people.

But I was tired of doing that.

I stayed in my seat.

This bus driver said to me,

"I'm going to have you arrested."

"You may do that," I said.

And I stayed in my seat.

Two policemen came.

One asked me,

"Why didn't you stand up?"

I asked him, "Why do you push

us black people around?"

The policemen took me to jail.

They took my picture.

They put my fingers on a pad of ink

and rolled my fingers

onto white cards.

That way, they had my fingerprints.

Then they put me in a jail cell.

I did not have to spend

the night in jail.

My husband came to get me.

A friend paid my bail money.

That meant I could go free for now.

The police told me

to come to court in three days.

I went to court.

The judge said I was guilty

of breaking the law.

I was fined ten dollars,

plus four dollars in court costs.

I never paid it.

I did not feel I had broken the law.

I thought black people

should not have to give up

their seats on the bus

to white people.

I thought the law should treat

black people and white people

just the same way.

I always wanted rules to be fair,

even when I was small.

HOW I GREW UP

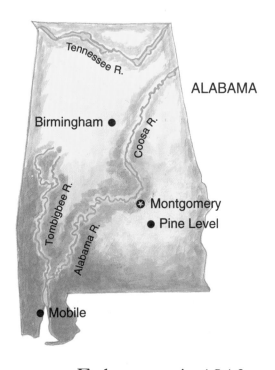

I was born on February 4, 1913.

I grew up in a place

called Pine Level, Alabama.

I was named Rosa Louise McCauley,

after my grandma Rose.

My little brother was named
Sylvester, after my grandpa.
My mother's name was Leona.
She was a schoolteacher.
My father was a builder of houses.
His name was James.

We lived on a farm
with my grandma and grandpa.
They owned their own land,
and grew vegetables
and raised chickens on it.

I liked to go fishing
with Grandma and Grandpa.
They could not see very well,
so I would put the worm
on the hook for them.

Pine Level was too small to have
buses or public water fountains,
or even a library.
But there was segregation
just the same.

Sylvester and I went

to a school for black children.

It had only one room.

White children went

to a bigger school.

There was a school bus
for the white children.
There was no school bus for us.
Sometimes when we walked to school,
the bus would go by
carrying the white children.
They would laugh at us
and throw trash out the window.
There was no way to stop them.

One day a white boy named Franklin

tried to hit me.

I picked up a brick,

and I dared him to hit me.

He went away.

My grandma was angry.

She told me not to talk back

to white folks.

I thought I was right to talk back.

When I grew up, I married

a man named Raymond Parks.

The year was 1932.

He was a barber.

He lived in the city

of Montgomery, Alabama.

I was proud of my husband

because he worked

to help black people.

He helped get lawyers for people

who had been arrested.

I began to work

to help black people too.

I wrote down their stories

when they were hurt by whites.

I asked young black people

to try to use the white library.

It was very hard work.

It was also very sad work,

because nothing we did really helped

make our lives better.

Then came that day on the bus
when I would not give up my seat
to a white person.
I was tired of black people
being pushed around.
Some people think I kept my seat
because I'd had a hard day,
but that is not true.
I was just tired of giving in.

28

WE STAY OFF THE BUSES

Many black people heard
that I had been arrested.
They were very angry.
They thought it was time
to fight for new laws.

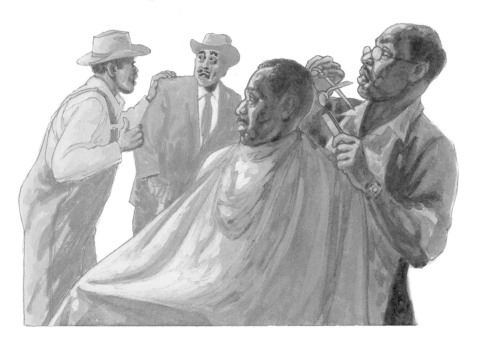

A woman named Jo Ann Robinson
said we should not ride the buses
if we had to give up our seats
to white people.
She passed out leaflets
asking all black people
in the city of Montgomery
to stay off the buses for one day.
This was called a boycott.

The day of the boycott came.

The buses were almost empty.

Very few black people were on them.

A man named E. D. Nixon

called a big meeting of black people.

The meeting was held in a church.

A young minister named

Dr. Martin Luther King, Jr.,

told all the black people

to keep off the buses.

Everyone at the meeting cheered,

and the boycott went on.

We walked to work or took taxis.

We got rides from our friends.

But we did not ride the buses.

Christmas passed.

It was very cold,

but we did not ride the buses.

White people were very angry.

They wanted us

to ride the buses again.

Some black people

even lost their jobs

because they would not ride the buses.

Some black people were arrested.

Some were beaten up.

I got telephone calls

from people who would not

give their names.

They said they wanted to hurt me.

Spring came.

Now it was nice weather for walking.

All the black churches

had station wagons

to drive the people

who could not walk.

Summer came.

The buses had stopped running.

There were not enough riders
without the black people.

Mr. Nixon and Dr. King got lawyers
to take our case to court.
They took our case
all the way to the Supreme Court
in Washington, D.C.
The Supreme Court said
that the segregation laws were wrong.
Black people should not
have to give up their bus seats
to white people.

Our boycott worked, and we had won.

We went back to the buses at last.

We did not have to give up

our seats anymore.

We had stayed off the buses

for a whole year.

SINCE THE BOYCOTT

Many white people were angry

that we had won.

My brother was worried

about our safety.

My husband and I left Montgomery

to find work and be near my brother.

We moved up North,

to Detroit, Michigan.

My mother moved with us.

Back in the South,

Dr. Martin Luther King, Jr.,

decided to fight against segregation

in other ways.

He led black people in the fight

to vote and to eat in restaurants,

just as white people did.

He was fighting for their rights.

This fight was called

the civil rights movement.

Some white people joined the fight.
Most went down South from the North.
But some white people in the South
joined the civil rights movement too.

I helped out by making speeches.
I told about being arrested.
I went down South
for some of the big marches
for black people's rights.
The civil rights movement
won many rights for black people.
New laws for equal rights were passed.
The old segregation laws were over.

Today I still make many speeches,
and I receive many awards.
Some people say I started
the whole civil rights movement
because I would not give up
my seat on the bus.

I know that many people
started the civil rights movement.
And many people worked very hard
to win the rights
that black people have today.
But I am glad that I did my part.

There is still much work to be done.
The laws that kept
black and white people apart
have been changed.
But there are still many people
who have not changed their hearts.

I hope that children today

will grow up without hate.

I hope they will learn

to respect one another,

no matter what color they are.